Native Americans

Tlingit Indians

Suzanne Morgan Williams

Heinemann Library
Chicago, Illinois

© 2003 Heinemann Library
an imprint of Capstone Global Library LLC.
Chicago, Illinois

Customer Service 888-454-2279

Visit our website at www.heinemannlibrary.com

All rights reserved. No part of this publication may be reproduced or transmitted in any form or by any means, electronic or mechanical, including photocopying, recording, taping, or any information storage and retrieval system, without permission in writing from the publisher.

Photo research by Alan Gottlieb
Maps by John Fleck
Production by Que-Net Media
Printed and bound in China by CTPS

15 14
10 9 8 7 6 5 4 3 2

Library of Congress Cataloging-in-Publication Data
Williams, Suzanne, 1949-
  Tlingit Indians / Suzanne Morgan Williams.
      v. cm. -- (Native Americans)
Includes bibliographical references and index.
Contents: Southeast Alaska -- Traveling to the sea -- The Ravens and the Eagles -- Villages and clans -- Living from the land and sea -- Clan art -- A Tlingit year -- Celebrations -- New people -- Sickness and change -- Taking land and treasures -- Alaska Native Brotherhood -- Modern and traditional -- The Tlingit future.
   ISBN 978-1-4034-0868-6 (lib. bdg.) -- ISBN 978-1-4034-4176-8 (pbk.)
   1. Tlingit Indians--Juvenile literature. [1. Tlingit Indians. 2. Indians of North America--Alaska.] I. Title. II. Native Americans (Heinemann Library (Firm))
   E99.T6W56 2003
   979.8004'972--dc21

                         2003007477

Acknowledgments
The author and publisher are grateful to the following for permission to reproduce copyright material:
pp. 4, 5 ©Macduff Everton/Corbis; p. 6 Kim Heacox/The Image Bank/Getty Images; p. 7 Barbara Brundage/Accent Alaska; p. 8 American Museum of Natural History Library/Neg.#338688; p. 9 Christie's Images/Corbis; p. 10 Alaska State Library/Neg.#PCA 87-1; p. 11 Alaska State Library/Neg.#PCA 87-10; p. 12 MCSUA/University of Washington Libraries/Neg#NA3945; p. 13 Alaska State Library/Neg.#PCA 87-106; p. 14 MCSUA/University of Washington Libraries/Neg#NA3854; p. 15 Burstein Collection/Corbis; p. 16 Alaska State Library/Neg.#PCA 87-197; pp. 17, 19 American Museum of Natural History Library/Photo by Emmons/Neg.#338436s; p. 18 Courtesy of the Bancroft Library/University of California, Berkleley; p. 20 Alaska Sate Library/Neg.#PCA 20-143; p. 21 Kennan Ward/Corbis; p. 22 MCSUA/University of Washington Libraries/Neg#NA2192; p. 23 MCSUA/University of Washington Libraries/Neg#NA2506; p. 24 David Muench/Corbis; p. 25 Alaska State Library/Neg.# PCA 20-98; p. 26 Courtesey Sheldon Jackson College/Stratton Library; p. 27 Alaska S tate Library/Neg.#PCA 274-1-2; p. 28 Jennifer Ortiz/Tundra Times Photograph Project/Tuzzy Consortium Library; p. 29 Jon Chase/Harvard News Office, © 2001 President and Fellows of Harvard College.; p. 30 Mark Kelley

Cover photograph by Vince Streano/Corbis

Special thanks to Mark (Hans) Chester and Roy Iutzi-Mitchell for their help in the preparation of this book.

Every effort has been made to contact copyright holders of any material reproduced in this book. Any omissions will be rectified in subsequent printings if notice is given to the publisher.

Some words are shown in bold, **like this.** You can find out what they mean by looking in the glossary.

Contents

Southeast Alaska

A bear walks along a stream. The stream spreads out and flows to the beach. Waves wet the stones and rocks along the shore. They shine in the late afternoon sun. Three **killer whales** jump and dive in the sea. **Ravens** squawk from a **cedar** tree. The bear moves toward the forest, looking for berries to eat.

This is southeast Alaska. Tlingit Indians live here and in the northwest part of Canada. Their **ancestors** learned to live in the mountains, in the forest, and by the sea. The Tlingit people are a part of this place.

The Tlingit Name

The word *Tlingit* is pronounced "KLINK-it." The Tlingit language does not sound like English. It has different sounds. The Tlingit language uses written marks such as **accents** and periods to tell readers how to say each word.

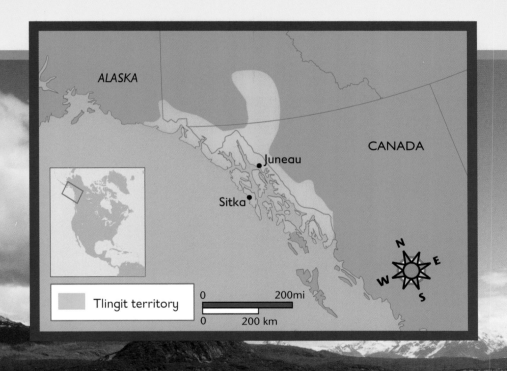

ALASKA

Juneau

Sitka

CANADA

N
E
W
S

Tlingit territory

0   200mi

0   200 km

5

Traveling to the Sea

Tlingit people say they came to southeast Alaska a long time ago. Thousands of years ago, ice covered much of present-day Alaska. Tlingits lived in the mountains, far away from the sea. They heard about a place with many fish. They decided to go there. They walked for a long time. Finally, they came to a huge **glacier.** No one knew how to cross it.

There are thousands of glaciers in the state of Alaska.

The tunnel under the glacier might have looked like this.

Then they found a tunnel under the glacier. A
river ran beneath the ice, but it looked dangerous.
Four old women offered to help. They paddled a
boat under the glacier and came out safely on the
other side. Then the Tlingits knew the way was safe.
They continued toward their new home by the sea.

The Ravens and the Eagles

Introductions
It is polite to introduce Tlingit people with their Tlingit name, moiety, and clan.

Tlingit people lived, worked, and traveled in **clans**. Clans are groups of relatives who help each other. A clan is a big family. Tlingit clans are divided into two groups, called **moieties**. The moieties are named **Ravens** and Eagles. When Tlingit children are born, they become part of their mother's clan and moiety.

Clan hats tell what clan Tlingits are a part of.
The people in this 1895 photograph are at a celebration.

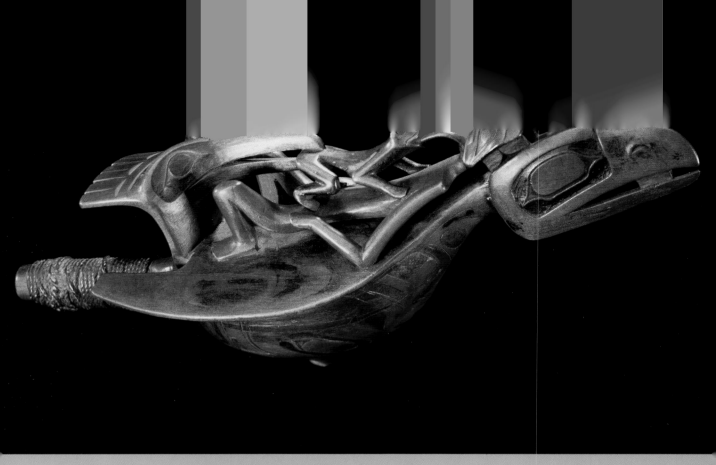

*Tlingits **carve** many objects. This is a wood rattle in the shape of a raven.*

In the past, Ravens married Eagles. Eagles married Ravens. Tlingits never married someone from their own moiety. Ravens and Eagles did certain jobs for each other. They helped when a family needed a new house or when someone died. Clans and moieties are still important to the Tlingits. But the rules about marriage and jobs are not always followed today.

Villages and Clans

Tlingits say that long ago when they reached their new home by the sea, different **clans** went in different directions. They built villages all along the coast. Men built clan houses with boards made from **cedar** or other trees. Each clan lived in its own large house. If the house got too crowded, some people built a new one.

*This photograph of a Tlingit village was taken in 1895. Some of the houses are **traditional,** and some are modern.*

*Some Tlingit houses were very big. This is the house of a Tlingit leader. The **carvings** show **clan symbols** and stories.*

When Tlingits married, someone had to move. The wife moved into her husband's clan house. Soon, members of many clans lived in each village. Tlingit travelers were welcomed at their clan's house in other villages.

In Their Own Words

"Cousins from the same **moiety** call each other brother and sister. They are very close. There is never anyone who is alone."

—Mark (Hans) Chester of the Coho Clan from the Far Out by the Ocean House, Frog House, Tlingit, 2002

Living from the Land and Sea

Tlingits got everything they needed from the land and sea. Men hunted seals and sea otters, and they caught fish. They hunted deer, rabbits, and bears. Men **carved canoes** from **cedar** trees. Women cooked berries and other foods. They **wove** baskets, clothing, and rain hats. Women also prepared animal skins for clothes. Some families had **slaves** who had been taken from other **tribes.** They helped with this work.

Tlingits were good traders. They used large canoes like this one to travel in the ocean. This picture was made in 1786.

These Tlingit women are weaving baskets from the roots of spruce trees.

The Tlingit people also had time to make beautiful things. They decorated their houses, canoes, and clothing with **clan symbols. Clans** owned many things. Each clan owned its houses and a fishing area. Clans call the important things they own *at.óow. At.óow* are used in clan celebrations.

In Their Own Words

"We are as one with our **ancestors** and children. We are as one with the land and animals."

—Rosita Worl of the Shangukeidi Clan from the House Lowered from the Sun, Tlingit, 1997

13

Clan Art

Tlingit artists create *at.óow,* or things that are important to the **clans.** A clan leader might ask an artist to **carve** a **totem pole.** He asks that the totem pole tell a story or something about the clan's history. Some women make *chilkat* **weavings.** They weave **cedar** bark and wool into clothing. *Chilkat* weavings are used for **ceremonies.**

Many people work together to carve a totem pole.
This photograph was taken in 1939.

The Tlingit Bear clan's leader wore this hat. You can see the bear clan symbol.

Totem poles and weavings are decorated with **clan symbols.** Only clan members can use the symbols. Each symbol has a story or meaning. Today, Tlingit carvers and weavers are known around the world.

Clan Names

Clans are named by where they are from. Clan symbols are often birds, fish, or animals. They are written here in English and Tlingit.

Beaver	*Deisheetaan*
Killer Whale	*Dakl'aweidí*
Wolf	*Kaagwaantaan*

A Tlingit Year

Today, as in the past, Tlingit children learn all year long by watching and doing. Boys learn from their uncles. Girls learn from their grandmothers, mothers, and aunts.

In Their Own Words

"Your uncles and aunts educated you because your father or your mother would be too easy on you."
—Kevin Skeek of the Chookaneidí Clan from the Ice House, Tlingit, 2001

Many Tlingit people still hunt and fish for part of their food. In the spring, Tlingits hunt seals. They also catch fish. They fix hunting gear and tools.

*This woman is **weaving** a chilkat **robe**. Most of the weaving was done in the winter.*

This 1889 photograph shows a Tlingit summer fishing camp.
The fish were hung up on racks to dry.

In the summer, families often move to hunting
or fishing camps. They catch salmon and hunt.
Women and children pick berries and gather eggs.
Today, Tlingits have jobs and go to school. This
means that now they may go to their camps on
weekends or for vacations. In the past, winter was
a time for **ceremonies,** storytelling, and getting
together in the villages.

Celebrations

A celebration called a *koo.éex'* helps Tlingits remember important things. In the past, it was also an important way for the **clans** to share things they owned. Some Tlingit families were rich and others were not. Powerful Tlingit clan leaders shared with everyone at a *koo.éex'*.

Tlingit Women

Clan women passed clan knowledge to their daughters. The clan leaders were the sons of important women in the clan.

Tlingits dressed up for koo.éex' celebrations. Many times these celebrations honored a marriage or a death.

Chilkat **robes** are worn at gatherings such as k̲oo.éex'. *This photo was taken in 1901.*

One clan held the k̲oo.éex', but the whole village came. Clan members from other villages came, too. Clans gave away many gifts. Everyone danced, ate, and listened to stories. People were honored, buried, or married at a k̲oo.éex'. The guests' job was to remember what happened.

New People

Tlingits say that the first white people came to southeast Alaska in the 1770s. Traders came from Russia, England, Spain, and the United States. They wanted furs from sea otters and other animals. Russian traders built **forts** near the Tlingits. But the Tlingits did not want Russians on the land. In 1802, many Tlingits fought the Russians. They destroyed a Russian fort at Sitka.

This 1805 painting shows Sitka. It was one of the first towns that Russians built on Tlingit lands.

20

Sea otter furs are very soft. They were worth a lot to traders.

In 1804, Russians attacked the Tlingits who lived near the fort. These Tlingits walked many days to a new camp. They told other Tlingit people not to trade with the Russians. In 1805, another group of Tlingits destroyed a Russian fort near their village.

Sickness and Change

Things changed after traders and missionaries came to Alaska. Europeans brought new **diseases** to Tlingit villages. Many Tlingits died from these diseases. The Russians and Europeans got sick and died, too. Others were killed in battles or decided to go home. Many missionaries stayed. They wanted the Tlingits to become **Christians**.

Family Names

Missionaries from the United States called Tlingit families by new names such as Tom, Paul, or Fred. Today many Tlingit families have these kinds of last names.

These Tlingit men and women worked for a fishing company. The photograph was taken around 1908.

This photo of Tlingit children was taken at an Indian boarding school around 1888.

In 1867 the United States paid Russia for the land where Tlingits and other native groups lived. This became the state of Alaska. People from the United States came. They built towns, **canneries,** and lumber camps near Tlingit villages. The United States government sent Tlingit children to **boarding school.** The children had to speak English and wear European-style clothes. The government did not let Tlingits have *k̲oo.éex'* **ceremonies.** Tlingit life was changed.

Taking Treasures

Tlingits shared the land. But in the 1880s, the United States government divided up Tlingit land. It gave or sold the land to single owners. Some Tlingits got land. But it was not as much land as they needed to live on. Many Tlingits did not get any land. The government sold some land to lumber companies, businesses, and miners. In 1902 the United States government took more Tlingit land. The government created the Tongass National Forest. Tlingits could not use that land, either.

Later, the United States government paid Alaskan **tribes** for the land in the Tongass National Forest.

24

Collectors took at.óow, totem poles, and clan house decorations from villages like this one.

In the 1890s and early 1900s, scientists and art collectors visited southeast Alaska. In the summer, Tlingits were away from their villages at summer fishing camps. The collectors thought that no one lived there. They took *at.óow,* **totem poles,** and **clan** house decorations to far-away museums and universities.

Alaska Native Brotherhood

In 1912 leaders from the Tlingits and other Alaskan **tribes** formed the Alaska Native Brotherhood. They wanted to help their people learn to live with the changes. They thought the people in their tribes should learn English. Leaders hoped this would help their people work with **settlers.** Many Tlingits stopped teaching the Tlingit language to their children.

The Alaska Native Brotherhood and Sisterhood work for the rights of Indians. This photograph was taken around 1914.

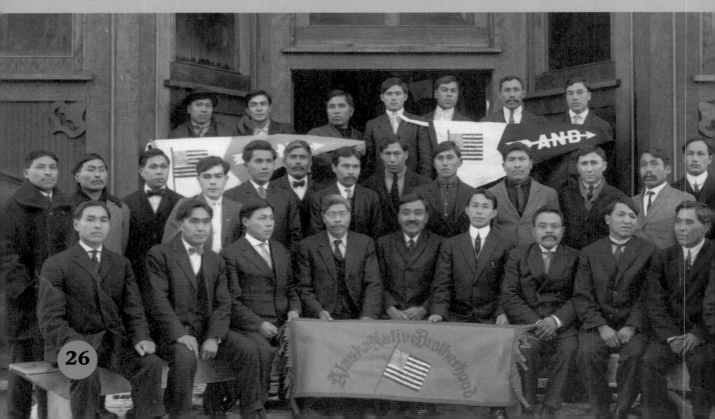

The governor of Alaska signed the state's anti-discrimination law in 1945. Elizabeth Peratrovich is second from the left in this picture.

White settlers did not always treat Indians fairly. They did not let Alaskan natives send their children to public schools or use certain hotels and restaurants. Elizabeth Wanamaker Peratrovich was a Tlingit. She belonged to the Alaska Native Sisterhood. She pushed the Alaska state government to pass an **anti-discrimination law.** The law opened restaurants, hotels, and housing to Alaskan natives. It was the first law like this in the United States.

Modern and Traditional

Today's Tlingit people speak English. They work in all kinds of jobs. Many Tlingits live in cities in Alaska, Washington, and other states. Others live in small villages as their **ancestors** did. They may know everyone in town. Many Tlingits still hunt and fish for some of their food.

*Tlingits are keeping their traditions alive. These Tlingits are celebrating with the **raven** dance.*

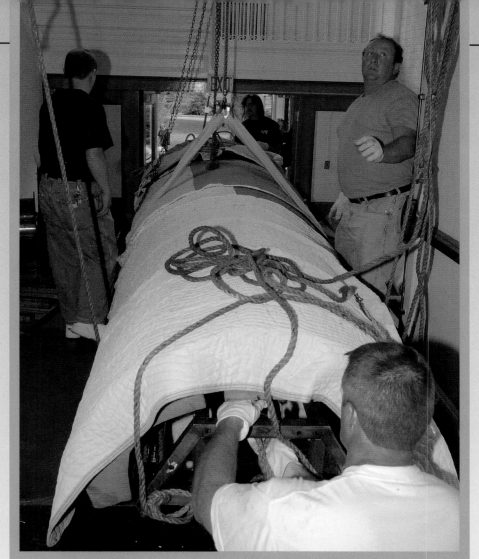

*These men are packing up a **totem pole** at a museum near Boston. It was returned to the Tlingit people in 2001.*

The Tlingit people are passing on their **traditions.** Tlingit leaders have brought some *at.óow* back to Alaska from far-away museums. New **carvers** and **weavers** are working today. Tlingit children are learning the Tlingit language. They can go to camps where they learn about the Tlingit way of life.

The Tlingit Future

Today, many Tlingit children have mixed family backgrounds. They may have a parent or grandparent who is not Tlingit. Tlingit children go to movies, use computers, and ride skateboards. But they are also part of a **clan**. They learn Tlingit **traditions** from their families. They learn to respect the land and the sea. They are Tlingit. They are the future.

Alaskan natives gather for a long weekend every two years. A big parade usually happens on Sunday.

Glossary

accent   written mark that means your voice goes higher on that syllable

ancestor   relative who lived long before someone's parents and grandparents

anti-discrimination law   law that says all people must be treated in the same way

boarding school   school where children live

cannery   factory where food is put into cans

canoe   narrow boat pushed along with paddles

carve   cut into a shape with a knife or sharp tool

cedar   large, brown-barked tree that grows in the Pacific Northwest

ceremony   event that celebrates a special occasion

Christian   person who follows a religion based on the teachings of Jesus

clan   group of families that are related

clan symbol   animal or object that stands for a clan

disease   sickness

fort   building with strong walls for defending against an enemy

glacier   large, slow-moving sheet of ice

killer whale   black-and-white whale with teeth

missionary   person who teaches others about religion

moiety   half of the Tlingit tribe

raven   large, black bird

robe   long, loose piece of clothing

settler   person who makes a home in a new place

slave   person who was bought and sold as a worker

spruce   kind of evergreen tree

totem pole   special carving that tells a story or history

tradition   custom or story that has been passed from older people to younger people for a long time

tribe   group of people who share language, customs, beliefs, and often government

weave   lace together threads or other material. A weaving is something made in this way.

More Books to Read

Ansary, Mir Tamim. *Northwest Coast Indians.* Chicago: Heinemann Library, 2000.

Brown, Tricia. *Children of the Midnight Sun: Voices of Alaska's Native Children.* Portland, Ore.: Alaska Northwest Books, 1998.

Staub, Frank J. *Children of the Tlingit.* Minneapolis, Minn.: Carolrhoda Books, 1998.

Index

STO

FRIENDS
OF ACPL

9/03

D1449502

CURT SCHILLING

JAY BELL

STEVE FINLEY

ANDY BENES

CRAIG COUNSELL

LUIS GONZALEZ

MARK GRACE

MATT WILLIAMS

TONY WOMACK

DEVON WHITE

BRIAN ANDERSON

RANDY JOHNSON

THE HISTORY OF THE
ARIZONA DIAMONDBACKS

JOHN NICHOLS

CREATIVE ⚫ EDUCATION

Published by Creative Education, 123 South Broad Street, Mankato, MN 56001

Creative Education is an imprint of The Creative Company.

Designed by Rita Marshall.

Photographs by AllSport (Al Bello, Jonathan Daniel, Jeff Gross, Tom Hauck, Jed Jacobsohn),

Associated Press/Wide World Photos, Icon Sports Media (John Cordes),

Sports Gallery (Al Messerschmidt), SportsChrome (Rob Tringali Jr., Michael Zito)

Copyright © 2003 Creative Education. International copyright reserved in all countries.

No part of this book may be reproduced in any form

without written permission from the publisher.

Library of Congress Cataloging-in-Publication Data

Nichols, John, 1966- The history of the Arizona Diamondbacks / by John Nichols.

p. cm. — (Baseball)   ISBN 1-58341-199-2

Summary: A team history that highlights the 1998 beginning of the new major league

baseball franchise in Arizona.

1. Arizona Diamondbacks (Baseball team)—History—

Juvenile literature. [1. Arizona Diamondbacks (Baseball team)—History.

2. Baseball—History.] I. Title. II. Baseball (Mankato, Minn.).

GV875.A64 N53 2002   796.357′64′0979173—dc21   2001047857

First Edition 9 8 7 6 5 4 3 2 1

THE STATE

OF ARIZONA IS HOME TO SOME OF THE MOST STRIKING

landscapes in the United States. From the stark radiance of the

Sonoran Desert in the state's southern half, to the painted beauty of

the Grand Canyon in the north, Arizona has it all. There are few

places on Earth where a person can play golf under a hot summer

sun in the morning and then drive to a snow-capped mountain for

an afternoon of snowboarding, but Arizona is one of them.

The capital of Arizona is Phoenix. Known as the "Valley of the

Sun," the area in and around Phoenix offers citizens and visitors a

wide variety of things to see, including museums, parks, and the

Phoenix Zoo. In 1998, a new attraction was brought to Phoenix—

a major league baseball team. The new franchise was named the

ANDY BENES

Diamondbacks in honor of the rattlesnakes native to the desert region.

{HOME AT THE BOB} Although the Diamondbacks did not

In **1995**, the Diamondbacks' ownership team paid $130 million to add their franchise to the NL.

begin play until 1998, the state of Arizona had been a friend to major league baseball for decades. Big-league teams had made the state the home of their spring training camps since 1947. By the early 1990s, eight teams conducted their spring training in the warm, dry air of Arizona.

In 1995, major league baseball looked for sites to place two expansion teams. With its established base of loyal fans, Arizona was an easy choice. On March 9, 1995, baseball announced that its two newest big-league cities would be Phoenix and Tampa, Florida, with Arizona placed in the National League (NL) Western Division and Tampa in the American League (AL) Eastern Division. After the decision was announced, Arizona businessman and Diamondbacks

JAY BELL

Speedy center fielder Devon White represented Arizona in the **1998** All-Star Game.

DEVON WHITE

owner Jerry Colangelo could not hide his happiness. "It's been a long road to get here, but now the team is a reality," he said. "All I feel is excitement for the future."

The new team needed a home, and a special one at that. Summer temperatures in Phoenix can rise as high as 115 degrees Fahrenheit. To ensure the comfort and safety of fans and players, unique features would have to be incorporated into the new stadium. With that in mind, the $354-million Bank One Ballpark—or "BOB," as it is affectionately known to fans—was built.

The retractable-roof stadium gave Arizona fans the best of both worlds. For blistering hot day games, the sliding roof was closed, and air conditioning cooled things down. At night, the roof was opened, and Diamondbacks fans enjoyed baseball under the desert sky. The stadium also included a decidedly unique feature.

Left-handed pitcher Brian Anderson was Arizona's top selection in baseball's **1997** expansion draft.

BRIAN ANDERSON

3 1833 04402 1753

Built at a cost of $354 million, the BOB was one of baseball's most extravagant parks.

BANK ONE BALLPARK

When an Arizona player hit a home run, water cannons located

behind the outfield fence blasted streams of water 35 feet into the

air to celebrate the round-tripper.

The Diamond-
backs ran
off seven
consecutive
wins in **1998**,
tying an
expansion-
team record.

{**DIAMONDBACKS TAKE THE FIELD**} Before the

Diamondbacks' first season, most baseball experts

expected them to suffer the same fate as most

expansion teams—a lot of losing. Arizona would not

break with tradition, as the team endured its share of expansion

heartache in 1998.

Despite the rough going, manager Buck Showalter knew he had

several pieces of a contending team in place. Unlike most expansion

teams of the past, the Diamondbacks had two distinct advantages

working for them: free agency and an owner willing to spend

money. Before their first season, the Diamondbacks signed a core of

talented veterans to help instill a winning mentality in the team.

MATT WILLIAMS

Among the veterans picked up were pitcher Andy Benes,

shortstop Jay Bell, third baseman Matt Williams, and center fielder

Devon White. Benes was an established ace pitcher, having previously

won 18 games in a season with the St. Louis Cardinals; Bell and

Williams gave the team great defense and potent bats in the middle

of the lineup; and the aging but still swift White was a dangerous leadoff hitter. "It's important that we bring quality people in to build the foundation of our franchise," explained Colangelo. "We put a lot of thought into these moves."

Pitcher Andy Benes came within two outs of pitching a no-hitter against the Reds in **1998**.

Along with these veterans, the Diamondbacks were also counting on production from some promising young players. Rookie first baseman Travis Lee and pitcher Brian Anderson would both play major roles in Arizona's first campaign.

14

After a terrible 9–31 start in 1998, the Diamondbacks began to put things together. Big seasons from White (22 homers and 22 stolen bases), Benes (14 wins and a 3.91 ERA), Lee (.269 average and 22 homers), and closer Gregg Olson (30 saves) allowed Arizona to finish its first season with a 65–97 mark.

{ARIZONA LANDS THE "BIG UNIT"} Most expansion teams are content to build their franchise over the course of four or

TRAVIS LEE

five years. Not so for the Arizona Diamondbacks. Encouraged by its

solid finish to the 1998 season, Arizona was one of the most active

participants in the free agent and trading markets prior to the

1999 campaign. The Diamondbacks signed fleet center fielder

Steve Finley and star pitcher Todd Stottlemyre. They also traded

with the Pittsburgh Pirates for speedy infielder Tony Womack and acquired hard-hitting outfielder Luis Gonzalez in a trade with the

Detroit Tigers.

While all of these trades and signings made

headlines, one free agent signing in particular rocked

the baseball world—Randy Johnson, perhaps the most

feared pitcher in baseball, was coming to Arizona.

The 6-foot-10 and 230-pound left-hander had spent a

decade blowing away hitters with his 100-miles-per-hour fastball

and wickedly snapping slider. Having spent the majority of his

career with the Seattle Mariners, Johnson was traded to the

Houston Astros during the 1998 season. After finishing the year in

Houston, the "Big Unit," as he was known, became the biggest prize

on the free agent market. "We told Randy we were building a

champion in Arizona and we needed his help to get there," said

Showalter. "When you can get a guy as dominant as he is on your

In his first season with the Diamond-backs (**1999**), outfielder Steve Finley scored 100 runs.

STEVE FINLEY

Utility player Craig Counsell was part of one of the NL's best defensive infields.

team, you jump at the chance."

With a reloaded lineup and a pitching staff that featured three

standout starters, the Diamondbacks were no longer

expansion pushovers. The team began the 1999 season

hot and stayed that way. Gonzalez led the way early on

with a 30-game hitting streak. "Gonzo," as he was

affectionately known to fans, proved to be the season's

In addition to his major-league-leading 72 steals, Tony Womack smacked 10 triples in **1999**.

most pleasant surprise. His .336 average, 26 homers, and 111 RBI

were all career bests.

Along with Gonzalez, the Diamondbacks received monster

seasons from just about every player in their lineup. Williams, Bell,

and Finley each blasted more than 30 home runs and drove in more

than 110 runs, while Womack led the majors in steals with 72. On

the pitching front, Johnson put together another stellar season. He

went 17–9 while leading the league with 364 strikeouts and 12

TONY WOMACK

complete games—an effort that earned him his second Cy Young

Award as the league's top pitcher.

With their star-studded lineup hitting on all cylinders, the

Diamondbacks captured the NL West title with a record of 100–62.

In doing so, Arizona became the first expansion team to ever

capture a division title in only its second year of competition.

{SNAKES IN THE POSTSEASON} The Diamondbacks' 1999 postseason opponents were the New York Mets, and Arizona had home-field advantage. In game one, Randy Johnson took the mound in front of 49,584 Diamondbacks fans at the BOB. The game was a tight affair, with the Mets taking an early 4–1 lead only to have Arizona rally to tie the game on home runs by Gonzalez and first baseman Erubiel Durazo. The game remained deadlocked until the ninth inning, when the Mets' Edgardo Alfonzo hit a grand slam to beat the Diamondbacks 8–4.

In game two, Todd Stottlemyre gave a heroic pitching perform-ance for Arizona. Stottlemyre—who had battled back from a mid-season arm injury—and the Arizona bullpen gave up only five New York hits, while Steve Finley drove in five runs to lead the Diamondbacks to a 7–1 victory.

In **1999**, catcher Kelly Stinnett hit one of the longest home runs at the BOB, a 456-foot shot.

KELLY STINNETT

Infielder Erubiel Durazo batted .329 after being called up from the minors in **1999**.

ERUBIEL DURAZO

The series then moved to New York. After the Mets pounded out a 9–2 victory in game three, Arizona pitcher Brian Anderson held New York to only two runs over seven innings in game four. Still, going into the top of the eighth, Arizona was down 2–1. Then, with two men on, Jay Bell crushed a pitch off the top of the wall—just inches shy of a three-run homer—for a two-run double that gave the Diamondbacks a 3–2 lead.

Veteran right-handed hurler Todd Stottlemyre led the Diamondbacks to their first postseason win.

25

Unfortunately for Arizona fans, New York came back to tie the score in the bottom of the eighth and sent the game into extra innings. In the bottom of the 10th, Mets catcher Todd Pratt homered off Arizona reliever Matt Mantei to clinch the game and the series for New York. "It's a big disappointment for all of us," said a somber Bell after the game. "Baseball hurts sometimes, but we have an awful lot to be proud of this year."

TODD STOTTLEMYRE

The early knockout in

the 1999 playoffs left the Diamondbacks eager to take a step for-

ward in 2000. But Arizona's much-anticipated third season turned

out to be a step backward instead, as injuries and inconsistency

plagued the franchise throughout the year.

The first crippling blow came when Williams broke a bone in

his foot during spring training. Injuries also sidelined Stottlemyre, Mantei, Lee, and Durazo for chunks of the season's first half.

Weakened but unwilling to give up, the Diamond- backs picked up the slack behind such replacements as first baseman Greg Colbrunn, infielder Craig Counsell, and reliever Byung-Hyun Kim. By the All-Star break, ailing Arizona had fought its way into first place in its division.

Known to fans as "Gonzo," Luis Gonzalez drilled 31 homers and knocked in 114 runs in **2000**.

Encouraged by the gutsy first-half performance, the team's front office decided to acquire some help for the pitching staff. In late July, the Diamondbacks sent three players to the Philadelphia Phillies for star pitcher Curt Schilling. During his nine previous seasons, Schilling had earned a reputation as one of baseball's most dominant hurlers. He won 14 or more games five times and twice led the NL in strikeouts. "With Curt and Randy, we are going to

LUIS GONZALEZ

have a great chance to win every game they pitch," said catcher

Damian Miller. "That's a great confidence booster."

An unsung hero, catcher Damian Miller got the best out of the team's pitchers in **2000** and **2001**.

Despite the addition of Schilling, the enormous amount of energy the team used to fight through the season's first half seemed to catch up with the Diamondbacks. Arizona faltered down the stretch and finished in third place at 85–77.

{HIGH HOPES IN THE DESERT} A few weeks after the 2000 season ended, Buck Showalter was replaced as manager by former big-league catcher and broadcaster Bob Brenly. The Diamondbacks then made a major off-season move by signing former Chicago Cubs first baseman Mark Grace. The 36-year-old Grace, a career .308 hitter and four-time Gold Glove winner, gave Arizona another proven veteran to count on in the middle of the lineup. "I could have signed with a lot of teams," said Grace, "but at this stage of my

DAMIAN MILLER

career, I want a shot to win the World Series. That's why I'm here."

Grace's decision proved to be a wise one, as the Diamondbacks

captured the NL West crown with a 92–70 record in

2001. In the postseason, Arizona defeated the St.

Louis Cardinals and Atlanta Braves to advance to the

World Series against the three-time defending cham-

pion New York Yankees. Arizona captured the first

Outfielder Danny Bautista batted .583 and drove in seven runs during the **2001** World Series.

two games at home but then suffered three straight losses in

New York. Two of those losses were heartbreakers in which the

Diamondbacks surrendered ninth-inning leads just one out away

from victory.

Back in front of their raucous fans at the BOB for game six, the

Diamondbacks routed the Yankees 15–2 to set up a dramatic game

seven. Down 2–1 in the ninth inning, Arizona rallied to defeat the

Yankees 3–2, winning the game on a bloop single by Luis Gonzalez.

DANNY BAUTISTA

Curt Schilling finished second in the **2001** Cy Young Award voting after going 22–6.

CURT SCHILLING

The "Big Unit," Randy Johnson, captured his third straight Cy Young Award in **2001**.

RANDY JOHNSON

The victory made Arizona the fastest expansion team to ever win a

World Series title and triggered a wild, state-wide celebration. "We

Known for
his sidearm
throwing
style, Byung-
Hyun Kim
was Arizona's
closer of
the future.

went through sports' greatest dynasty to win our first

World Series," exclaimed Schilling, who won three of

the four games for Arizona.

In just a few short years, Arizona has risen from its

roots as a spring training stopover to become the

home of a major-league powerhouse. The Diamondbacks have taken

their lumps and are now in position to dole them out. For all oppos-

ing teams looking for a win in the Valley of the Sun, a warning sign

should be posted: "Beware of the snakes!"

BYUNG-HYUN KIM